HELPING CHILDREN DEAL WITH ANGER

Jenny Mosley and Helen Sonnet

Permission to photocopy

This book contains materials which may be reproduced by photocopier or other means for use by the purchaser. The permission is granted on the understanding that these copies will be used within the educational establishment of the purchaser. The book and all its contents remain copyright. Copies may be made without reference to the publisher or the licensing scheme for the making of photocopies operated by the Publishers' Licensing Agency.

Acknowledgements

This is the second book we have produced with LDA in the Helping Children Deal with … series. Corin has been our editor throughout this series and for many other books besides. He is extraordinarily calm and wise. When we get pent up and fail to put our theories into practice, he is always there to remind us quietly. Thank you, Corin, for sharing your skills and talents with us. LDA is a wonderful company to work with. We have particularly valued the support and expertise of Cathy Griffin and Debbie Risley on this project and others.

The rights of Jenny Mosley and Helen Sonnet to be identified as the authors of this work have been asserted by them in accordance with sections 77 and 78 of the Copyright, Designs and Patents Act 1988.

MT10014
ISBN-13: 978 1 85503 411 2
© Jenny Mosley and Helen Sonnet
Illustrations © Dusan Pavlic
All rights reserved
First published 2006
Reprinted 2007

Printed in the UK for LDA
Abbeygate House, East Road, Cambridge, CB1 1DB, UK

CONTENTS

Introduction 4

Conducting Circle Time 8

Looking at emotions 10

Looking at emotions in others 12

Seeing anger positively and realistically 16

What happens to my body when I feel angry? 19

How anger can explode 21

Lighting my fuse 23

Looking at angry actions 25

Calm and angry 27

Looking at triggers 29

How our anger can affect others 31

Looking at the effects an angry outburst can have on our bodies 33

Looking at ways to calm down 36

What makes your fuse longer or shorter? 39

I can make a difference 41

Change the script 43

Conclusion 47

Resources 48

INTRODUCTION

Are any of these scenarios familiar? Do you encounter children who need help with dealing with anger appropriately? If so, then this book will help both them and you.

Chloe stared at the numeracy problems she had been asked to complete. 'What's the point of this rubbish? I hate maths,' she snapped. 'Every day maths and more maths. Well, I'm not doing it and you can't make me! I can't stand school and I can't stand you!' She kicked her chair back and stalked past the teacher, out of the room.

On the way to school Tariq's brother had wound him up by taunting him, leaving Tariq feeling angry, frustrated and in a bad mood. Then his teacher was sharp with him for not settling down to work sooner. 'Leave me alone,' Tariq shouted, and swept his work off his table. That felt good, so he pulled all the books off the nearby bookcase, threw them on the floor and kicked over several unoccupied chairs. The other children watched in frightened silence.

In the playground, a small group of boys were teasing Jack. They knew exactly the right ways to annoy him. After several minutes of their jeers and name-calling, Jack's composure cracked. He rushed at the group with his arms and legs flailing.

These three scenarios show the devastating effects that uncontrolled anger can have, on both the child expressing their anger inappropriately and the people around them. Violent outbursts can cause physical hurt to others and be deeply upsetting to all who witness them.

How to use this book

This book is designed to be a very practical resource. It contains a wealth of activities that can be incorporated into your Circle Time sessions or delivered as part of your curriculum provision for SEAL (Social and Emotional Aspects of Learning) and PSHE. The materials also include useful stories, poems and scripts for small dramas and scenes.

Each activity in the programme is designed to build on the one before it. This should help children develop their understanding and skills systematically. However, if you do not want to run an in-depth programme or if you have a specific need, you can select the activities and sections that you feel are of particular relevance.

Who is this book for?

This book is for headteachers, teachers, teaching assistants, learning mentors – in fact, anyone who leads groups and wants to help children learn the skills of anger management. The sessions are designed to give children a comprehensive understanding of how anger functions and how everyone has different triggers and responses to the feelings that anger stirs up. The inclusion of art, drama, poetry and many active games ensures that the concepts grab children's attention and are memorable as well as educational.

Why children need this book

Children often have very little understanding of the subtleties of cause and effect when it comes to anger. It is seen as an involuntary response that is beyond their control – 'It's not me, it's my temper!' This can be particularly true of children with quick tempers who may feel demoralised by the negative consequences of their frequent eruptions. Anger may involve the loss of self-control, and many children are appalled at the things they have said and done after the event. Sometimes, it is too late to make adequate recompense and the child discovers that their anger has cost them friendships, privileges and, importantly, trust.

Having established this, it is important to note that anger is a healthy emotion and can be a natural response to circumstances that we find ourselves in. Everyone feels anger. Sometimes, it is this emotion that gives us the energy to defend ourselves and those we love when we feel violated or experience injustice. Indeed, anger has provided the motivation for people to tackle such issues as civil rights abuses, apartheid, famine and poverty.

Children need to learn when to express anger, how to express it responsibly and safely, and how to control its expression. This book explores the concept of triggers – those things that are likely to provoke irresponsible anger in us. There are activities that will help children to recognise their triggers and the physical changes that occur when anger begins to rise. There are opportunities to investigate strategies to defuse anger, leading children to an understanding that they are responsible for their behaviour and they can exercise control over how they act. This will help them to be more aware of the destructive force of inappropriate anger and the way in which it can increase tension.

While anger is an acceptable emotion, the behaviour that accompanies it may not be acceptable. However, if children do not learn suitable ways to express anger, it will creep out in unsavoury ways. Changing unsuitable angry behaviour is not easy. Some of your children may enjoy the short-term rewards of power and status that their angry outbursts bring. However, with a persistent focus on the beneficial effects of change, by using the activities in this programme they can learn effective long-term strategies for successful relationships and friendships, and begin to see their positive impact on their future.

By the end of this programme, children should be able to make the following statements:

- I can recognise when I'm becoming angry.
- I understand the triggers for my anger.
- I use calming strategies.
- I know what to do to cope with others' anger.
- I can speak assertively.
- I can appreciate other people's point of view.
- I can get on with others.

Before beginning the programme, you may want to ask the children to fill in the table on page 6. You can repeat this exercise at various points during and after the programme to monitor the progress being made. The table on page 7 will be useful to review your own progress as you work through the programme.

Coping with my anger checklist

Read each of the sentences in the table. For each statement decide whether you do what it says always, sometimes or never. Be honest about your choices. Put a tick in the appropriate box.

Name:	Always	Sometimes	Never
I can recognise when I'm becoming angry.			
I keep myself calm in difficult situations.			
I recognise the triggers that make me angry.			
I speak assertively.			
I get on with others.			
I appreciate others' points of view.			
I know how to cope with others' anger.			

© *Helping Children Deal with Anger LDA* Permission to Photocopy

---

Coping with my anger checklist

Read each of the sentences in the table. For each statement decide whether you do what it says always, sometimes or never. Be honest about your choices. Put a tick in the appropriate box.

Name:	Always	Sometimes	Never
I can recognise when I'm becoming angry.			
I keep myself calm in difficult situations.			
I recognise the triggers that make me angry.			
I speak assertively.			
I get on with others.			
I appreciate others' points of view.			
I know how to cope with others' anger.			

© *Helping Children Deal with Anger LDA* Permission to Photocopy

Keeping your help effective

Look through the following questions to find out where you need to explore your views on anger and to reflect on your conduct. As you progress through the programme you will find that your expertise in areas in which you are weaker will improve.

	Yes	No
Do you accept that people have different anger thresholds?		
Do you understand that children need help and encouragement in order to learn how to deal with their anger in appropriate ways?		
Have you devised individual action plans for children who need specific help?		
Have you given adequate praise and reward to children for trying to deal with their anger in positive ways?		
Have you taught your children effective calming techniques?		
Have you taught your children new things to say and ways to act in challenging situations, and given them the opportunity to practise these?		
Do you have appropriate negotiated rewards and sanctions in place?		
Have you encouraged your children to take responsibility for their behaviour?		
Are you leading by example in managing your own anger in a positive way?		

© *Helping Children Deal with Anger LDA*   Permission to Photocopy

Conducting Circle Time

To conduct the Circle Time sessions in this book, it is good to have a grasp of the stages of a Circle Time as part of the Quality Circle Time model.

Meeting up – playing a game

Always try to start a Circle Time with an engaging warm-up activity.

This helps everyone to relax in each other's company. It helps if the game involves the children changing places so that the group is well mixed up. This opens up the opportunity for new friendships and stronger group dynamics.

Warming up – breaking the silence

In a Circle Time, everyone has the right to speak and the responsibility to listen.

This stage should be a round in which a short sentence stem is used, such as 'My favourite meal is ...'. The leader introduces this stem, which continues round the circle until it gets back to them. They complete the stem for the final time.

A small speaking object, such as a painted wooden egg or a soft toy, is used to show who is speaking. The person holding it has the right to speak without interruption. The object is passed to the next person once the current holder has finished. Any child who does not wish to speak may say 'pass' and hand the object on.

Some children may say 'pass' because they are not sure what to say or because they are being uncooperative. Try to tell your group what the round is going to be about the day before so that they have a chance to prepare. They can jot their sentence down on a card if necessary.

As the speaking object is holding me ...

If you work with very young children who may be shy, it may help to hold a number of smaller circles beforehand. You can use a puppet to talk about the forthcoming Circle Time. A child can tell the puppet their sentence and, if needed, the puppet can speak for them in the main circle.

Opening up – exploring issues

This is the most challenging stage of a Circle Time, when important issues are explored in an open forum.

It may include discussion, role play, creative activities and puppets to help explore an issue more deeply. This is the phase in which new skills can be learnt, new insights reached and intentions shared.

Cheering up – celebrating the positive

This stage is used to affirm the group's work in the open forum and in their time together generally.

It should be a positive and happy time that can be used as a way to highlight the effective use of the strategies learnt.

Calming down – bringing children forward

Using a ritual to bring a Circle Time to a close helps to make the transition to the next part of the day calm and peaceful.

You could do this by playing a very quiet game, listening to relaxing music or using a guided visualisation.

This gives the children space and time for the learning of the open forum to sink in.

These five stages are the foundation of the Quality Circle Time model.

For the Circle Times in this book we have focused on the opening-up stage to show how this can be used to explore anger in an accepting environment. We have included a game to draw each session to a close.

LOOKING AT EMOTIONS

In this session, children explore how our emotions are made clear physically, such as in facial expressions, speech and body language. While what we say and how we say it give obvious clues to how we are feeling, understanding body language is vital to good communication and relationships.

Learning goal

I can identify, recognise and express a range of emotions appropriately.

Resources

A picture book containing illustrations of a character showing different emotions. A set of photographs of children showing a range of feelings, such as the 2005 DfES SEAL whole-school resource file, is useful. LDA's 'Emotions' (1996), a set of photo cards showing a range of emotions, is a good resource.

What to do

Opening activity

Prepare by making a list of the ways in which we express our emotions so that you can prompt the children if necessary. If you have carried out the earlier stages of a Circle Time, thank the children for their input so far. If not, ask them to sit in a circle and greet them in a cheerful manner. Ask them how they think you are feeling. Choose children to make some suggestions such as happy, excited, and so on. Ask them to say what clues they picked up that indicated how you were feeling. These could include comments such as these:

- 'You are smiling.'
- 'Your shoulders are relaxed.'
- 'Your eyes are bright.'

At the end of this part emphasise that a person's expression and body show the emotion that they are feeling.

Repeat this to explore a sad, an angry and a frightened expression.

Make sure that you give positive feedback to children's comments and observations.

Going deeper

Put the children into pairs, and name one child in each 'A' and the other 'B'. Explain that you are going to give the pairs a scenario. Child A will show their partner how they would feel in that scenario through facial expressions and body language. Child B reports back to their partner what they observed about their expressions and posture. Child B then acts out the next scenario that you give them.

The following scenarios should get you started:

- You have opened the best present you've ever received.
- It's the middle of the night and you hear a strange noise.
- Someone has broken a treasured possession / favourite toy.
- Your mum/dad told you off for something you didn't do.
- You walked home a different way and now you are lost.
- Your mum/dad shrunk your favourite T-shirt in the wash.
- You've just heard that you are going on holiday to a fantastic destination next week.
- You think someone else is treated better than you at home/school.

Ask for volunteers to act out one of the scenarios to the rest of the group. Ask the other children to tell you the physical signals that indicate how the child is feeling. If you have a flipchart to hand you could record the children's observations for later use.

Time to reflect

Show the children the picture book that includes a character showing different emotions. Point out that just as we learn to read the written words of a story, we need to learn how to 'read' people's expressions and body language. Reflect on the skills explored in this session by discussing what emotion the character is expressing in each of the pictures.

Apply the skills of reading people's emotions to the photo cards, if used. You could display the images that you look at, with the children's comments written alongside. This will help to reinforce and remind children to apply the skills they have learnt.

Ask for volunteers to explain why the ability to 'read' other people's emotions is a very useful skill. Repeat these back to the group and praise the contributors for their thinking skills. Suggestions might include so that we can . . .

- . . . understand other people better;
- . . . get along as a group;
- . . . learn how to cope with other people's emotions;
- . . . learn how to cope with our own emotions;
- . . . enjoy ourselves and have fun together.

Closing activity

Finish the open forum with a round using the sentence stem: 'One thing that makes me feel happy is . . .'. Ask the child on your left to complete this stem. This process continues round the circle until the stem gets back to you. You complete it for the last time.

Extension activity

Collect from newspapers and magazines a range of photographs of people showing different emotions. Put the children in different pairs and give each pair a photograph. Ask them to look at their image and annotate it to show how they can tell which emotion(s) is being experienced.

The final pieces of work could form a display alongside the photo card work.

> **Action plan**
>
> Make a resolution to smile at the children at every possible opportunity. This really does have an amazing effect on morale.

LOOKING AT EMOTIONS IN OTHERS

This session consolidates the work on how we can read other people's emotions and begins to explore how we can respond in appropriate ways. Anger is not covered here as it is explored in detail in subsequent sessions.

Learning goal

I can recognise the feelings of others and explore a range of suitable responses.

Resources

A list of situations for the children to respond to. This could include such scenarios as these:

- A friend has just found out that they have won a competition.
- Someone in your family has lost something special to them.
- You make a friend jump as a joke, but they burst into tears.
- A child in the playground is looking sad and lonely.
- One of your friends has some new trainers that another friend has wanted for ages.

What to do

Opening activity

Gather the children into a circle. Revisit the previous session by asking some children to mime an emotion. Focus on the primary emotions of anger, fear, sadness and happiness. You may want to cover some secondary emotions such as being jealous, frustrated, proud, nervous, calm, excited, and so on. You could whisper the emotion to the child before they mime it so that the other children do not know what it is before they see the actions. After each mime ask the other children what emotion was being acted out and what the clues that they saw were.

Children with low self-esteem often lack confidence, which can lead to their being angry and aggressive or quiet and withdrawn. It is hard for them to understand and express their emotions easily. It might be a good idea before a session like this to use a hand-held puppet with a small group that includes such children. The puppet can introduce the theme and explain what is going to happen. If a child doesn't want to speak in the session, they can give their answer to the puppet so that it can speak for them when their turn comes.

Action plan

Explore the use of puppets in Circle Time. They provide a useful vehicle to explore emotions.

Going deeper

Explain to the children that our emotions tell us how we feel, and our expressions and body language tell others how we are feeling.

Discuss the scenarios on your list in turn. Begin by brainstorming how you could tell what emotion the person is feeling in the situation, consolidating the work just covered.

The next stage is to explore how the children think they should respond to the person. This could include how they might act, what they might say and what they might do. Here are some suggestions:

A friend has just found out that they have won a competition

- Congratulate them.
- Ask them to tell you all about it.
- Smile and show that you are excited for them.
- Shake their hand / give them a hug, if they're happy with this.
- Accompany them to tell other people.

Someone in your family has lost something special to them

- Suggest where they might look, ask them to retrace their steps.
- Give them a hug or hold their hand, if they're happy with this.
- Look at them directly with a kind expression as they tell you.
- Help them to look.
- Offer some kind words of support such as 'I'm sorry you lost ... and that you're feeling sad.'

You make a friend jump as a joke, but they burst into tears

- Apologise for upsetting them.
- Explain that it was meant as a joke.
- Find them somewhere quiet to sit down, if that helps.
- Ask them if they'd prefer to be on their own for a while.
- Find them a tissue if they need one.

A child in the playground is looking sad and lonely

- Ask them if they want to join in your game.
- Find a playground friend / lunchtime supervisor to help them.
- Ask if something has upset them.
- Find someone for them to play with.
- Offer to sit with them for a while and keep them company.

One of your friends has some new trainers that another friend has wanted for ages

- Admire your friend's new trainers when your other friend is not around.
- Give your other friend some space to work through their jealous feelings.
- Get both your friends involved in a game.
- Spend some time talking to the friend without new trainers if that would help them.

Time to reflect

Explain how being able to read a person's emotional state can provide much information, helping us to understand how they are feeling and to make decisions about how to respond appropriately.

Closing activity

Finish the open forum by sending a big, happy smile round the circle. Choose a child to start. They turn to the child on their left and give them a cheerful smile. The smile is then passed round in this manner until the person who started the round receives a smile from the child on their right.

Extension activity

Use spare moments to revisit points. Either act out an emotion yourself or ask a child to do so, and then ask the children to explain how they could tell how you were feeling. Ask for suggestions for how they might help a person who is feeling in that way.

Share the poem 'The Smile Starter' with the group. Use it often to remind children of the contagiousness of a smile and its beneficial effects. You could give children a photocopy of the poem to decorate and display.

The Smile Starter

Smiling makes you happy

When you are feeling blue.

When someone smiled at me today

I started smiling too.

I passed around the corner

And someone saw me grin,

When he smiled I realised

I'd passed it on to him.

I thought a lot about that smile

And realised its worth –

A simple, little smile like mine

Could travel round the Earth.

So if you see a smile begin,

Don't leave it undetected,

Share that smile with everyone

Let no one be neglected.

Source unknown

SEEING ANGER POSITIVELY AND REALISTICALLY

In this session, the children investigate how humans instinctively respond to a threat and how such a response can have benefits. They will also explore how controlled anger can motivate us to make positive changes on a personal and community level.

Learning goal

I know that anger is a strong emotion. If I take careful notice of it and use it appropriately, it can have positive effects.

Resources

Try to gather some reference materials on our early human ancestors and on reformers such as William Wilberforce, Martin Luther King and Bono.

What to do

Opening activity

Ask your group to form a circle. Talk about a time when you watched a wildlife programme and saw two angry lions / mountain goats / crocodiles confront each other. Ask the children what they think happened. They are likely to say that one ran away or that they fought. Ask them if they can give any examples of either of these responses from their experiences of the animal kingdom – these could be from films, documentaries or books.

Tell the children that they have just described what is called the fight or flight response. This is a term devised by the American scientist Walter Cannon, and describes our body's primitive, automatic response that prepares us to fight or flee from a perceived threat.

In the past, this response was vital to our ancestors' survival. For the purposes of this activity we shall refer to such ancestors as cave people. Tell the children that cave people usually lived in small family groups or tribes. They were often in danger from other tribes and predators.

This shows the fight or flight response explored by Walter Cannon.

Going deeper

If this is not a suitable activity for your group, leave it out as it is important to keep the session emotionally safe.

Ask the children to explain some of the risks such people may have faced, such as attacks from predators, lack of shelter, threats from other tribes, disease and so on. For risks that presented immediate danger the fight or flight response was important for survival.

Ask the children to help you to make a list of questions they would ask a caveman or cavewoman if they were able to travel back in time. Assume that the caveman or cavewoman is able to respond effectively to the questions.

Put the children into small groups. Ask them to prepare a short role play in which they pretend they are a camera crew that has gone back in time to make a documentary about cave people.

HELPING CHILDREN DEAL WITH ANGER

Give each person in the group a role such as camera operator, sound recordist, interviewer and caveman or cavewoman. Add further roles if necessary. Ask the groups to think of a few questions that investigate how dangerous life was at that time and how the fight or flight instinct helped people to defend themselves.

After giving the groups time to devise questions and to practise their role play, call them back to the circle and let each group act out their interview.

Remember that some children don't find it easy to perform in front of others. If you have groups including such children, you or a group member could observe their role play during the practice and report back on what took place.

Time to reflect

Revisit the ways in which anger may have helped cave people to survive – giving them the courage to defend themselves, to act quickly and to decide when to retreat. Lead the children into considering how they would have needed to use their anger in a controlled way.

Bring the positive aspects of controlled anger up to date by talking about how anger has motivated people to work for change. You could mention the following:

- Anger prompted Martin Luther King to make a stand for civil rights in the United States.
- Anger prompted William Wilberforce to seek the abolition of slavery in the UK.
- Anger prompted Bono to become involved in poverty action and third world debt.

Conclude by saying that anger is a healthy emotion that can help and empower us, but we need to learn to channel it to help us and to manage it as there is a danger of its getting out of control.

Action plan

Find out about people who have channelled their anger to promote positive change. Are there any campaigns run by charities that you could become involved in as a group?

Closing activity

Sort the children into pairs and ask them to stand opposite each other. One child is to make an angry face. The other child has a minute to ask their partner questions to which they have to answer 'Sausage' without laughing. If they succeed or when a minute elapses, they swap roles. The more bizarre the question, the better. For example:

- What are you wearing on your head?
- What do you brush your hair with?
- What's your favourite vegetable?

Extension activity

Explain that traditionally face paint was used as a way to make people look fierce. Give each child a copy of the face template on page 18 and ask them to decorate it to look angry and threatening. This is a good way to revisit the work done on understanding angry facial expressions. The artwork produced during this activity will create an eye-catching display.

If you show children some painted faces as examples, try to include a selection from a range of cultures.

Face template

WHAT HAPPENS TO MY BODY WHEN I FEEL ANGRY?

This session focuses on the physical aspects of anger, helping children to recognise the changes that usually occur in someone's body during a build-up to an angry outburst and the outburst itself.

Learning goal

I can recognise the changes in my body that tell me I am feeling angry.

Resources

A flipchart pad and a pen. You may need a large area for the opening activity.

What to do

Opening activity

This opening game reminds children of the work from the previous sessions on facial expression and body language.

Ask the children to move around the space pretending to be angry. They are not to touch anybody. If a child meets up with someone, they must each stand still, facing the other person and holding their angry expression. They must try not to laugh. Every 30 seconds or so, depending on how long you play the game, you say the words 'Move on', at which point any children standing still change direction and set off again. After a few minutes, bring the game to an end and ask the group to form a circle.

Going deeper

You might like to comment on the ways in which the children chose to move to express their anger. This is a good introduction to the discussion that follows. Say to the children that you could tell they were feeling angry by their expressions, body shape and movements. If you want to go into more detail you could mention such things as scowls, pursed lips, taut muscles, and quick and loud steps.

Tell the group that there are usually smaller clues to a feeling of anger. Ask the children to think of a time when they felt angry and to tell you how their body felt. List their comments on the flipchart. They are likely to suggest such things as:

- a dry mouth;
- a rapid heartbeat;
- a sick feeling;
- hot cheeks;
- feeling they were going to explode;
- sweaty palms;
- racing thoughts;
- rapid, shallow breathing.

Explain that our bodies really do change when we become angry. Our heart beats faster to send more blood and oxygen to our muscles, making them ready for action. There is a greater likelihood that we will act impulsively, leading to actions that we may regret afterwards.

Ask the children to reflect on the situations they thought about earlier in this activity. Request volunteers to say any of the physical characteristics from the flipchart list that they experienced in their situation. If they are happy to share the situation they were thinking about, that will provide a context for their comments.

Time to reflect

Stick a number of large sheets of paper together. Ask for two volunteers: one to lie on the paper and the other to draw round them. Place the outline in the middle of the circle.

Ask the group to think about where they experience anger in their bodies. Ask volunteers to come forward, one at a time, to mark a chosen place on the outline. If you have time, they could write or draw something that relates to their chosen area – for example 'sweaty palms' if they chose hands or a picture of a butterfly if they chose the stomach.

When you have a range of contributions, sum up by pointing to each place marked on the outline and describing the sensation that is often felt in that part of the body. For instance, point at the hands and describe how they may get clammy or sweaty and curl up into fists.

Thank the children for their contributions. Tell them that you will display the outline so that they can refer to it and use what they have learnt to spot their own anger when it appears.

> **Action plan**
>
> Supplement your display with text that describes the biological changes that occur when someone becomes angry.

Closing activity

End the session with a game. A leader establishes a steady two-clap rhythm. Once the rhythm is established, the leader pulls a face after the first set of two claps. The rest of the group has to copy this face. This pattern is then repeated several times. Be the leader yourself until the children become familiar with the game. After a few rounds, choose a confident child to take over as the new leader.

Extension activity

Ask the children to look in story books, comics and magazines for pictures of people feeling angry. When they find an example, they could mark the page with a Post-it® note and put the item in an agreed place in the room. After a few days, you can have a discussion in which volunteers come forward, show the picture(s) they found and describe the events that accompany the image(s).

HOW ANGER CAN EXPLODE

In this session, the children will consider how a build-up of tension can lead to an outburst of anger, and reflect on the unwelcome consequences.

Learning goal

I know that all emotions are fine, but that it is not right to behave in any way I feel like.

Resources

A balloon and a balloon pump, a flipchart, a marker pen, and a CD of sounds of nature such as running water.

What to do

Opening activity

You need the balloon and pump for this part of the activity. You can give the balloon a name. Try to choose a name that could be male or female, such as Ashley. As you attach the balloon to the pump, tell the children a few incidents from their day that have made them feel angry. You could include:

- being told off by their mum for having a messy bedroom;
- being late for school because their brother/sister wasn't ready;
- being called an unkind name by a classmate;
- breaking a new pen;
- dropping their snack on the playground.

Each time you mention an incident, pump some air into the balloon. Invite the children to think of other incidents and continue to pump up the balloon until it bursts.

Be sensitive about any children in your group who may have an aversion to popping balloons. You may have to warn them or make alternative provision for them.

Going deeper

Tell the children that this is what can happen when anger gets out of control – the emotions can get bigger and bigger inside us until we 'explode'. Ask the children what happens when people 'explode'. List their suggestions on the flipchart. They may say things like:

- attack someone physically – punching, kicking, scratching, hair pulling;
- shout;
- swear;
- become upset;
- go off in a sulk;
- ignore people;
- tell lies.

Put the children into small groups and tell them that they need to devise a mime or dance of a balloon growing and expanding until it is at the point of bursting, at which point they must freeze. Give each group one of the themes from the opening activity as a stimulus. Ask them to think about what may happen if the action continues and the anger bursts out.

After a short while, ask each of the groups in turn to show their mime/dance. After each mime, the group says what their stimulus was. Ask the children what they think might happen next. Write their suggestions on the flipchart. These could include positive (walk away) and negative outcomes (have a fight).

> **Action plan**
>
> Use the mimes or dances as part of a presentation in assembly to explore some of the things the children have learnt about anger.

Time to reflect

Explain to the children that if we are not careful our anger can burst out of us in an uncontrolled way or a 'big bang', as with Ashley. However, if we are aware of the feelings building up inside us we can learn ways to cope more effectively with our feelings and to let the hot air out in a controlled manner.

Closing activity

Ask the children to imagine that they are each a balloon that is going to be pumped up. They need to start from a tight, curled-up position on the floor. Each time that you make a pumping sound with the balloon pump, the children inflate a bit, enlarging their body shape. After several pumps, they should be near to bursting point. Ask the children to hold this position.

Take an imaginary pin and pop each inflated balloon that has been created. Each child can then rush around the room, making a wonderful noise and becoming smaller and smaller. Eventually all the children will be lying on the ground again. Now ask them to imagine that they are so relaxed that their limbs feel they are melting into the floor. You could use words such as the following:

Lie on your back, close your eyes and let your legs and arms feel heavy. Let the floor take their weight so that they feel they are sinking into a soft blanket. Now you are going to tense and then relax each part of your body in turn. Start by screwing your face up tightly, hold it and then relax it so it feels soft and loose. [Go through a range of body parts, tensing and relaxing, finishing with the toes.] *Now, when I count to 3, I want you to stand up slowly. 1 … 2 … 3.*

Some children may not be able to take part in the closing activity without sabotaging it. If you feel this may apply, use some soothing music to calm the group instead. Play the music while the children lie on the floor. If you use a CD of water sounds, for example, ask volunteers how many different water sounds they heard.

Extension activity

Give each child a piece of paper folded into four. Ask them to show the build-up of Ashley's anger in pictures. On the first three quarters they need to show Ashley getting progressively bigger and bigger. In the final quarter, they need to show Ashley bursting. They could add a key word to each quarter, such as **cross**, **angry**, **angrier** and **livid**. They could develop their pictures to tell the story of why Ashley felt so angry.

LIGHTING MY FUSE

In this session, the children share examples of situations and experiences that make them feel angry.

Learning goal

I know that feelings, thoughts and behaviour are linked.

Resources

A soft ball, a pin, a mug, and a photocopy of page 24 and pen for each child.

What to do

Opening activity

Ask the children to sit in a circle. You stand in the middle with the soft ball. Tell the children that you will throw the ball to each of them in turn. When a child receives the ball, they need to throw it back to you, at the same time saying one thing that makes them feel angry. If you think they might find this difficult, you can ask for examples from the children before you start. Tell them that it does not matter if someone says what they were going to say; it means they share the same feelings.

You can roll the ball in this activity if catching it will present a problem to your group.

Going deeper

Give each child a pen and a photocopy of page 24. Ask them to write some of the things that make them feel angry in school along the length of the fuse. They should not use other children's names in this activity.

Time to reflect

When the children have finished the work on the photocopied page, ask them what would happen if the fuse were to burn right down. The answer is likely to be that the dynamite will explode, placing everyone nearby in danger. Ask the children what would happen if the fuse were put out before this – no explosion, so everyone remains safe.

> **Action plan**
>
> Make a classroom display of the children's work on what makes them feel angry. You can use it to review how they are coping with these triggers later in the programme/term year.

Closing activity

Ask the children to make the same angry noise together, such as 'Aagh'. They need to start this noise quietly and increase the volume until it is as loud as possible. Ask them to repeat the process, watching you at the same time, as at some point you will give a visual sign, such as raising your hand, as a signal for them to become quiet again. Any child who fails to respond to your signal must remain quiet for two rounds, after which they can join in again.

Ask the children to sit on the floor, close their eyes and breathe in very calmly through their nose, if possible, as you count slowly to 3. Repeat the count as they breathe out. Repeat this a couple of times. Tell the children that you are going to drop a pin into a mug and that they need to listen for the sound. Ask the children to keep their eyes closed and raise their hand when they think they hear it.

Extension activity

Carry out the written activity for different contexts such as in the playground, playing with friends, at home, and so on.

Lighting my fuse

LOOKING AT ANGRY ACTIONS

This session introduces the idea that although anger is a normal and natural feeling, there are acceptable and unacceptable ways of expressing it.

Learning goal

I know that it is fine to have feelings, but not right to behave in any way I feel like.

Resources

A chair, a piece of paper and a pencil for each group.

What to do

Opening activity

Put the children into small groups and tell them that they are going to think about an imaginary child who often gets angry. You can give the child a name, but not one that the children will know from their group. Appoint an actor, a scribe and a spokesperson in each group. Ask the groups to tell their scribe the things the child might do when they felt angry. The scribe notes their suggestions, which could include:

- breaking or damaging property;
- hurting people physically;
- upsetting or frightening people;
- looking foolish in front of others;
- losing friends;
- receiving sanctions;
- losing privileges.

Going deeper

Choose a group to begin. Ask the actor to sit on a chair, representing the angry child. Ask the spokesperson to come forward and read one example from their list.

The child on the chair needs to take the example and put it in a sentence that describes what they need assistance with – for example, 'I need help because when I lose my temper I swear loudly.'

Ask all the other children to think of a suggestion to help the child control their anger. Then ask volunteers to give their suggestion using the sentence stem 'Would it help if you …'. Examples might include these:

- 'Would it help if you counted to 10?'
- 'Would it help if you gave someone a cuddle?'
- 'Would it help if you punched a pillow?'
- 'Would it help if you sat quietly somewhere?'

The children need to consider the specific details of the problem so that they can tailor their suggestions accordingly.

The child on the chair needs to thank everyone for their help.

After a few suggestions change to another group and repeat.

You may decide to use a puppet to represent the child feeling angry. They can be seated on the lap of a group member who listens to their whispered responses and speaks for them. You could even take the role of the child yourself.

HELPING CHILDREN DEAL WITH ANGER

> **Action plan**
>
> Ask the children if they can offer suggestions to help you when you feel angry.

Time to reflect

Reiterate that feeling anger like the actors expressed is normal. It is natural to feel anger at times. How we handle these feelings is very important. There are appropriate and inappropriate ways to behave when we feel angry. If we don't handle our anger well, we are likely to hurt ourselves and/or others.

Closing activity

End the session with a circle game called 'The tone of my voice' in which the children say 'Goodbye, everyone. I hope you have a nice day.' The group says the sentence in unison. Choose a different tone of voice for each time they say the sentence – for example, happy, sad, angry, lonely, excited.

Extension activity

The children write about or draw a cartoon strip telling the story of a child's angry behaviour. This needs to include the circumstances that made them angry, how the anger exhibited itself and the consequences of the behaviour.

For younger children the main character does not need to be a child. It may be easier if it is an animal or cuddly toy.

CALM AND ANGRY

In this session the children focus on the different emotional states associated with feeling calm and angry, using words, colours and shapes to express their ideas.

Learning goal

I can identify, recognise and express the emotional states of being calm and being angry.

Resources

Enough large sheets of paper for two per group, a range of coloured pencils or felt-tip pens for each group, two short pieces of music, one tranquil and the other loud, and a rainstick.

What to do

Opening activity

Tell the children that they are going to explore feeling calm and angry. Put the children into pairs or small groups, depending on how many you are working with. Give each group two large sheets of paper. Ask one child in each group to write 'Calm' at the top of one sheet and 'Angry' at the top of the other.

Tell the children they need to write or draw anything that they associate with each word on the relevant sheet. They can use words, colours, shapes, characters and so on to depict each emotional state – the more creative and inventive, the better.

Give the groups 20 minutes or so to do this work.

> **Action plan**
>
> This would be a good exercise to complete yourself, then show the children your ideas.

Going deeper

Make a frieze by joining all the sheets of calm associations together. Repeat this with the sheets of angry ones. Display these and spend some time with the children looking at each of them, picking out items of interest or common themes.

Time to reflect

Play the two contrasting pieces of music to the children. Ask them to describe how each piece made them feel. You could also discuss what images they brought to mind. Compare these comments and observations with those recorded on the friezes.

Closing activity

Finish this activity with the visualisation that follows. Keep your voice calm and quiet. Don't read too quickly.

Find a comfortable place on the floor to lie on your back and close your eyes. Imagine it's a warm day and you are lying on a beach. You can feel the warmth of the sun on your closed eyelids. There is a light breeze that stops you feeling too hot. Slowly you breathe in the wonderful air, full of oxygen and energy. As I count to 3, take in a deep breath though your nose. 1 . . . 2 . . . 3. Now, slowly breathe out the stale energy and the hot carbon dioxide. Keep breathing in and out as I count to 3. [Make a few repetitions.] As you continue to breathe, you feel the warmth of the sun on your shoulders, your chest, your knees, your legs and your feet.

I am now going to use a rainstick. As you listen to its sound, imagine the waves from the sea gently breaking on the pebbly beach. They are very soothing and match the speed of your breathing. Imagine that there is a huge bubble in front of you and put the picture of yourself on the warm beach inside it. Carefully blow the bubble so that it floats high above you and falls into your head to be stored as a happy memory to use at a time when you need to close your eyes and become calm. After I count to 3, I want you to open your eyes and smile at someone near to you. 1 … 2 … 3.

You can buy suitable relaxation CDs if you would rather use that option.

Extension activity

Find two other pieces of music, one calm and another stormy. Give the children paper, pastels and/or paints. Play them one of the pieces of music and ask them to draw/paint whatever abstract patterns or marks the music suggests to them. Repeat this with the second piece of music. Use the finished compositions in a display about the differences between angry and calm.

There is a range of story books about a character called Moppy, published by Positive Press. You could use *Moppy is Angry* (2003) and *Moppy is Calm* (2005) to support this session.

LOOKING AT TRIGGERS

In this session, the children consider that there are certain things, which we shall call triggers, that always make them angry. If they are aware of their triggers, they may be able to take steps to prevent an angry outburst.

Learning goal

I can recognise when I am becoming overwhelmed by my feelings.

Resources

A flipchart and a pen.

What to do

Opening activity

Ask everyone to sit in a circle. Ask the children to think about the things that always seem to make them feel angry. This is not the time to mention names if it is something that happens at school. Make a list of the suggestions on the flipchart. These may include:

- being called a nasty or silly name;
- being told off;
- being last in line for lunch;
- being told when to go to bed;
- not being allowed out to do something they want to do.

In the event of a disclosure that you believe is a child protection issue, you will need the support of your school's appointed officer. Make sure you know your LA's procedure.

Explain to the children that each of us has big or small things that frequently provoke our anger. These sorts of things are called 'triggers'.

Going deeper

Ask the children in what contexts they have heard the word 'trigger' before. Their suggestions are likely to be linked to weapons of some kind. Explore what a trigger does. Establish that it usually sets something in motion; in the case of a gun it's what causes it to fire. Ask the group why they think the word 'trigger' is used in association with anger. The intention is for them to understand that a trigger situation or action can cause their anger to fire off.

Even talking about our triggers can make us feel stressed, so handle the discussion with care. You may decide to use a story book or puppets as a safe starting point to explore this theme.

Time to reflect

Explain that recognising and knowing what their particular triggers are, along with the previous work on knowing how anger feels, can help them be more aware of flash points and learn ways to calm down before they fire off.

> **Action plan**
>
> Take time to think of your own triggers in the classroom. Write them down and think about why they make you particularly angry. Being aware of your triggers will help you to tackle them more effectively.

Closing activity

Ask the children to think of something that is a trigger for them. Perform a round using the following sentence stem: 'My trigger is . . . but I can choose not to fire.' Choose a child to begin the round and be sure to join in yourself.

Extension activity

Make a collection of all the strange phrases people use to describe feeling angry. Some examples are these:

- I was hopping mad.
- I saw red.
- I blew my top.
- I just exploded.
- I blew my fuse.
- I lost my rag.
- I went ballistic.
- I went wild.

Talk about how most of the expressions that people use are either explosive or involve an element of losing control.

You could give each child an expression to illustrate with a cartoon. These pictures could be used as part of a display on anger.

HOW OUR ANGER CAN AFFECT OTHERS

This session encourages children to reflect on the consequences of their angry outbursts.

Learning goal

I can stop and think before acting.

Resources

A flipchart and a pen.

What to do

Opening activity

With the children sitting in a circle, ask them how they feel when someone shouts at them. Tell the children that you are going to act angrily and ask them to do something.

Say the following in an angry tone: 'Bring me a cup of tea. I said I wanted a cup of tea. Bring me one, now!'

Ask the children how they might respond if someone spoke to them in such an angry way. These might include:

- shout back;
- be upset;
- be shocked;
- look for a way to get their own back;
- no longer be their friend.

Going deeper

Draw an outline of a person on the flipchart and write the children's suggestions around the figure.

Draw a second outline on another page of the flipchart and ask for suggestions for how they might respond to the same request if it were made in a pleasant way: 'Would you be really kind and make me a cup of tea now? Thank you.'

Ask the children which is the most useful way to get a cup of tea.

Time to reflect

Point out that anger hardly ever gets us what we want and often gets us the opposite. It is important to notice how people are reacting to our behaviour so that we can decide whether things are all right or if we need to modify our behaviour. We always have a choice about how we behave, even when we feel angry about something.

Action plan

Giving verbal praise to individuals and your group can do a great deal to promote positive emotions and self-image. Make sure that you regularly tell the children how brilliant they are and how pleased you are to have such a lovely group. It really works wonders!

Closing activity

Ask each of the children to think of words that describe how they like to be spoken to.

Perform a round using the following sentence stem: 'When people speak to me, I prefer them to be ...'. Choose a child to begin the round and join in yourself.

Extension activity

Tell the children that together you are going to look in more detail at how anger can affect other people. Sort the children into pairs. Ask each child in a pair to think about something that makes them angry when it is said to them. Ask them to avoid the use of any swear words or name calling. Give the children examples such as these:

- 'Get lost!'
- 'We've got enough players.'
- 'You can't borrow my ruler.'
- 'You're not my friend any more.'

In their pairs, each child is to say what they have chosen in an angry way a few times. This might be quite noisy.

LOOKING AT THE EFFECTS AN ANGRY OUTBURST CAN HAVE ON OUR BODIES

This session consolidates the work done on the changes in our bodies when we feel angry. This can help children deal with the aftermath of an angry outburst by themselves or someone else.

Learning goal

I can identify, recognise and express a range of feelings.

Resources

A flipchart and a pen.

What to do

Opening activity

Ask the children to sit quietly in a circle. Ask volunteers to describe how they feel sitting in this relaxed manner. If they have difficulty with this, get them to think about a time when they felt relaxed. They are likely to say such things as calm breathing, cool skin, smooth brow, slow or no movements, and so on.

Next, ask them to stand and to run on the spot for a minute – count the seconds slowly in your head. When you reach 60, tell them to stop. Ask them to tell you how different their bodies feel from when they were sitting quietly. Look for responses such as feeling hot, breathless, heart beating faster, legs feeling wobbly, sweating.

Going deeper

Remind the children that their bodies also change when they feel angry. Ask them what they can remember about what happens to their body when they feel angry. List the changes they mention on the flipchart. They will include changes such as rapid heart beat, rise in body temperature, lack of logical thought.

Explain to the children that because their bodies go through these changes during an outburst of anger, they are likely to feel differently afterwards. Ask them if they can remember how they felt after they had acted in an angry manner. You will probably receive replies such as tearful, exhausted, numb, shaken, unsettled. Explain that the body often feels like this after it has experienced an extreme emotion such as fear, excitement or anger.

Time to reflect

Tell the children that it can take up to 45 minutes for the body to return to a fully relaxed state after an angry outburst. Some feelings can linger for several days, and they might find themselves thinking about and reliving an incident for some time after it.

At the beginning of another lesson, tell the children that you are going to set an alarm clock for 45 minutes. When the alarm clock goes, stop the lesson and ask the children to think about what they have done in the last 45 minutes. Remind them that this is the length of time that it takes most people to calm down after an outburst of anger.

Being more aware of the negative impact of some angry events can help children to manage their anger more effectively. It can also help them to understand how someone may be feeling after they have displayed their anger inappropriately. Such insights can lead to better relations as the group will understand how to cope with each other's angry episodes and how/when to promote reconciliation. This will mean that the negative effects of an angry outburst will fade away more rapidly.

Closing activity

End with an enjoyable game to focus the children on something positive. Ask them to stand in the circle. Begin by performing a simple action, such as tapping your head with your hands. The children remain standing still. When you say 'Switch' and change the action, the children begin to copy the first action that you performed. Each time you shout 'Switch' and change your action, so do the children, but they are always one action behind you and need to concentrate on your movements closely.

> **Action plan**
>
> Look at the form on page 35. Use this when a child has reacted angrily, causing hurt and offence. By completing it, the child will review what made them angry, what they did when they were angry and any action(s) that is needed now that they have calmed down. Self-reflection of this nature is valuable for helping children to manage their anger effectively.

Extension activity

Ask the children to keep a feelings record for a specified time period, such as a day or a lesson. Give each child a piece of paper and tell them that you will ask them to record their emotions at specified intervals throughout the chosen time period. This could be once an hour, or every 10 minutes, depending on the period chosen. This could be as simple as drawing a face showing a smile, frown, tear, and so on, depending on how they are feeling.

This activity helps children to learn how to monitor their emotional state and to realise that it can change a lot in a short period of time.

Looking at my anger

I felt angry because ....
....
....
....
....

When I was angry ....
....
....
....
....
....

Now that I am calm, I should:

-
-
-
-
-

Next time I feel angry, I will:

-
-
-
-
-

HELPING CHILDREN DEAL WITH ANGER

LOOKING AT WAYS TO CALM DOWN

This session explores a variety of tried-and-tested techniques for calming down.

Learning goal

I know how to calm myself down when I feel angry.

Resources

A flipchart and a pen.

What to do

Opening activity

Begin this session with a round using the sentence stem 'I know when I am starting to feel angry because ...'. This is a useful way to recap on the changes that occur in the body when someone feels angry.

Going deeper

Ask the children to share any strategies they use to try to calm themselves down when life is stressful or they feel themselves becoming angry. Ask them to explain and, if appropriate, demonstrate their strategies so that the other children understand them and can try them in the future. Make a list of the suggestions on the flipchart. Your list might include:

- breathe deeply;
- repeat a calming mantra like: 'Cool, blue ocean';
- count slowly to 10 or backwards from 100;
- walk away;
- find somewhere to sit quietly.

Put the children into small groups. Give each group a calming technique from the flipchart and ask them to devise a short role play to show how it might work. Each group will need to think of a situation in which people might get agitated or angry, assign each other roles and then devise a scene that shows how their given technique 'rescues' them from getting angry and out of control. Offer guidance if the groups have difficulty thinking of ideas.

Would it help if you counted to 10, or possibly 1000?

You might like to stipulate that one child in each group acts as the anger officer who steps in if the situation seems about to get out of control and reminds the participants of their given calming technique.

Ask the groups to show their role plays.

Time to reflect

Discuss each strategy seen in the role plays. Ask the children to think about which technique(s) they will try next time they feel themselves getting angry. You could hold a review session in a couple of weeks to find out if they have used any new strategies and what the outcome was.

Closing activity

Stand in a circle and ask each child to join hands with the child on either side. Choose a child to begin the game. They gently squeeze the hand of the child on their left, who repeats this to the child on their left and so on until the squeeze has passed around the circle and back to the leader. Choose a different leader and repeat the game.

> **Action plan**
>
> Put the list of calming techniques in a prominent place so that everyone has a reminder of the strategies that they can use when they feel angry.

Extension activity

Remind the children of the calming mantra 'Cool, blue ocean'. Ask the children to think of other words that sound soothing and calm. They could discuss their ideas with a partner and/or use a suitable dictionary. Make a collection of these words on the flipchart and ask the children to pick out words to make a short mantra of their own. They could write their mantras on small cards and decorate them with restful colours. You could circulate these to other groups, classes and even parents.

A survey of well-known lullabies will provide a range of soothing and gentle words for the children to use in composing their mantras.

You could ask the children to design stay-calm posters that focus on the benefits of remaining calm. They can do this individually, in pairs or small groups. They might like to think of a slogan to use, such as 'Stay calm, anger harms'. These posters can be displayed around the school.

If you have a child who particularly needs to work on anger, you can enlist the help of the other children in your group. For a script that explains how to do this, see the next section.

Engaging peer support for an anger-management plan

You may have a child who particularly needs to work on managing their anger. An effective way to do this is to ask the other children in your group to join in helping them. Make sure that you discuss what follows with the child before you introduce the procedure to the group.

Gather the children together in a circle. When you reach the open forum of your Circle Time, explain that the whole group is going to work together to help the named child control their anger, which they are finding difficult at the moment.

Say that the named child is going to try really hard to stay calm, and it would be brilliant if the other children could think of ways to help them.

Give the children a few moments to think about something to say, such as a strategy for the child or something the other children can do. Hold a round to explore the ideas.

Use a speaking object, such as a painted egg or soft toy. Choose a confident child to begin the round. Give them the speaking object and ask them to complete the sentence stem 'Would it help if . . .'.

Possible responses include these:

- . . . I offered to be a special buddy and invited you to join in a game?
- . . . I didn't deliberately provoke you?
- . . . I made sure I said well done when you stayed calm?
- . . . you have a picture of an angry face that you show to us if you are feeling angry?
- . . . you had a safe place to go when you felt angry?

Devise an action plan with the children for how they should respond in a helpful way if the child becomes angry.

This could include the following:

- quietly ask the person to try to calm down;
- don't retaliate or act aggressively;
- give them some space;
- ask an adult to help;
- walk away;
- wait for the person to calm down before talking to them.

Record both lists on a flipchart.

When you have compiled the lists, ask the named child to decide which of the suggestions they think would be helpful and would like to try.

Tell the children that you will have another Circle Time in a week or two to review how the action plan is going. Work out a suitable whole-class reward that all the children can enjoy if the named child reaches their goal with the group's help. The goal might be an agreed number of anger-free days or examples of handling their anger appropriately.

WHAT MAKES YOUR FUSE LONGER OR SHORTER?

In this session the children consider the factors that may have an effect on their mood and make them more susceptible to feeling angry.

Learning goal

I know that how I'm feeling can have a positive or negative effect on my thoughts and behaviour.

Resources

A soft ball and a large copy of the following poem.

What to do

Opening activity

Read the following poem to the children.

I hope they let me play today

I hope they let me play today and they're not mean and rude.

If they say 'Go away!' again, I'll be in such a mood.

They're whispering as I approach and looking in that way

That tells me that I can't join in, just like the other day.

'Can I play with you?' I ask. She says, 'The game is full.'

My stomach churns, my face feels hot, I'm raging like a bull.

'One more won't hurt,' I say to her. 'You could just fit me in.'

'You're not our friend. We don't want you.' She gives a nasty grin.

I feel my anger rising up. I think I'm going to burst.

I don't know what to do or say, I feel as if I'm cursed.

'I hate you all!' I scream and yell. I push and kick and hit.

Mrs Maxwell's coming over, but I don't care a bit.

She quietly steps in front of me and gently takes my arm.

'Come with me,' she kindly says. Her voice is strong and calm.

She leads me to a quiet place. I sit and start to cry.

'What made you act like that?' she asks. 'Can you tell me why?'

'I couldn't help myself,' I say. 'I want to share their fun.

They wouldn't let me play with them. What else could I have done?'

When you have read the poem to the children, ask them to think of how else the child who wanted to join in could have behaved and what they could have said that might have resulted in a better outcome for everyone involved. Make a note of any suggestions you could return to in the next section.

Going deeper

Remind the children about the dynamite analogy used in the 'Lighting my fuse' session (page 23), if you have covered this. The analogy relates to how anger can explode suddenly and dramatically.

Explain that a stick of dynamite explodes when its fuse burns down. The length of the fuse dictates how long it is before the dynamite explodes. Discuss how we have different lengths of time before we feel angry – some people have quicker tempers than others. We use the explanation 'They have a short fuse' to describe someone who gets angry quickly.

In addition to our natural propensity to feel angry, explain that other factors can reduce the time before we feel angry – they can shorten our anger fuse. Ask the children to suggest factors. Suggestions might include:

HELPING CHILDREN DEAL WITH ANGER

- being overtired;
- feeling unwell;
- being worried about something;
- feeling down in the dumps.

Next, discuss what factors might have a beneficial effect – increasing the length of your anger fuse. These suggestions might include:

- having a good night's sleep;
- feeling healthy;
- feeling happy;
- sharing your worries with someone.

I think they both need a glass of water and a good night's sleep.

Time to reflect

In addition to these strategies for general well-being, ask the children to think of strategies to help to prevent them from losing their temper. Examples include these:

- Warn people when you are having a hard day.
- Don't expect too much of yourself on difficult days.

- Look for the positives in situations and people.
- Smile more.
- Treat yourself well – stand in the sunshine, read a favourite book, sit in your favourite chair.

Action plan

Make some feelings cards. Each card represents a feeling, such as happy, sad, angry, frightened, excited, thoughtful, embarrassed, jealous, calm. Provide several copies of each. At the start of the day a child chooses a card that relates to how they are feeling. They could attach their cards to a display showing their names. Allow them an opportunity to change their card at various times in the day. You will need to adjust the number of cards depending on the size of your group.

Closing activity

Stand in a circle facing inwards. You, or a child, stand in the centre holding a soft ball. As you throw or roll the ball to a child, tell them something that you wish or hope for them, such as 'I hope you have a happy lunchtime.' As they throw or roll the ball back, they say 'Thank you.' Your wishes or hopes should focus on things that will help the children feel calm and happy at school.

Extension activity

Refer to the poem used earlier in the session. Ask the children to think of a new ending that shows a positive resolution. They can communicate this new version as a story, a play script, a picture or a poem. Share these new versions with the rest of the group and discuss what strategies the different endings employed.

I CAN MAKE A DIFFERENCE

This session focuses the children's attention on how they can aggravate or calm a situation depending on how they react.

Learning goal

I know that my actions affect others and how they feel.

Resources

A flipchart and a pen, a pair of scissors, a plastic bag, a dictionary and a soft ball.

What to do

Opening activity

Explain to the children that people can either make a situation worse or better when someone is angry. Ask the children to suggest behaviour that is likely to make a situation worse. Record their suggestions on the flipchart. Leave space between statements as you will be cutting them up later. Statements may include:

- making fun of the person who is angry;
- provoking someone so they become angry;
- being deliberately uncooperative;
- shouting back;
- calling someone names;
- refusing to answer someone;
- egging someone on when they are angry;
- taking sides in a dispute.

Going deeper

Ask the children to think of ways that might help to calm an angry person/situation that they are involved with. Record these on another flipchart page as before. Examples might include:

- give a person who is angry some space;
- quietly ask the person to calm down;
- suggest an adult helps with the problem;
- maintain a non-aggressive stance;
- remove yourself from a dangerous situation;
- wait until the person has calmed down before talking about what happened;
- don't retaliate.

Cut the first list up so that each statement is on a strip of paper. Fold the strips up and put them in the plastic bag. Put the children into pairs or small groups. Ask each pair or group to come up in turn and take a piece of paper out of the bag.

Each pair finds an area to work in. They unfold their statement and read it to themselves. Help them if necessary. Give the pairs 15 minutes to devise a short mime to illustrate the statement on their strip of paper. Ask the pairs to come forward in turn, and show their mime. The other pairs are then asked to guess what was written on that pair's strip. You can discuss the likely outcome of each mime if it were to continue. Discuss what strategies from the second list might help the situation. Thank the children for their hard work.

Time to reflect

Ask the children if they know the meaning of the word **responsible**. Use a dictionary to help with this, if appropriate for your age group.

Refer to some of the mimes and ask the children to decide who was responsible for the outcomes in each mime. By exploring this, the children will be consolidating the learning point of this session, that their actions affect others and how they feel.

Closing activity

Stand in a circle facing inwards. Stand in the middle holding a soft ball. Throw or roll the ball to someone in the circle. As they return the ball, they say a word they associate with calm, such as **peace**, **cloud**, **float**, **stream**, **sleep**, **relax**, **smile**, **cushion**.

Extension activity

Write a class acrostic using the letters of the word **peace**. Write each letter one above the other on the left-hand side of the flipchart. Ask for suggestions to complete each line. Here is an example to get you started:

- Putting other people first
- Ending unkindness
- All working together
- Caring for one another
- Everyone being kind and helpful

Action plan

Use your class acrostic as part of your class code of conduct. Try the same activity with other words linked to this area, such as **calm**, to come up with other ways to remember key skills.

CHANGE THE SCRIPT

This session gives the children an opportunity to practise alternative ways of acting to responding angrily, helping them to appreciate there are more productive ways of behaving.

Learning goal

I understand that the way I express my feelings can change the way other people feel.

Resources

One photocopy of page 45 for each group. Plenty of space to work in. If you are working with younger children, you may prefer to use the story on page 46.

What to do

Opening activity

Give each group a photocopy of page 45. Read it through with the children. Don't discuss it at this point. If using the scenarios, put the children into groups of two or three, depending on which they will be working on.

If you are using the story, begin by reading it through with the group. The story explores the consequences of anger in an engaging way. You can use puppets to act out the story.

Going deeper

If you are using the scenarios, ask the children to spread out in their groups. Tell them which scenario each group is going to explore. Ask the children to look at their script and tell them to think of different sentences that will give the situation a positive outcome. In scene 1, the adult must be cross at the start; in scene 2 the teacher must be asking for silence; and in scene 3 child A and child C must be mocking child B. After that it is up to the group to rewrite the script in a positive manner. After 10 minutes or so, give the groups time to practise acting out both scenes. Bring the whole group back together and ask them to perform both the original and the alternative scene. If you have a large number of groups, you may have to do this over more than one session.

To follow up the story, ask the children what the animals' teachers could do to help restore the friendship. Rewrite the script with the children so that Caz explains to Mig how sad he is feeling, and Mig tells Caz how much he likes his old friend and how they should be kind to their new classmate. Act out the revised script with the puppets so that the children see the new ending.

Time to reflect

After you have watched some or all of the scenarios, ask the children who performed to describe how they felt after acting both versions. Talk about how learning more positive ways of responding to difficult situations can help them to avoid reacting angrily and the harmful consequences that might follow.

If you are using the story, tell the children that if we can control our anger, we can usually have a more positive influence by talking the problem through and listening to one another. Tell the children the important thing is to get an outcome that everyone can agree to, if possible, rather than to win the argument. Arguing can leave everyone upset, even if they feel they have won the argument.

Closing activity

Finish the session with a game called 'Pass it along'. In this game, the children sit in a circle. One child is chosen to mime passing an imaginary object to the child on their left. This continues until the object is returned to the child who began the round. Ideas for objects could include a kitten, a hot potato, a fragile glass ornament, a heavy box.

Action plan

Use the scenes you have worked on in this session as part of an assembly to show the other classes in the school what your group of children have been learning about anger and the positive outcomes that they have seen.

Extension activity

Ask older children to write some other play scripts of arguments. These can be exchanged between individuals or pairs and rewritten with positive outcomes.

Provide opportunities for younger children to use the puppets during the week to explore other scenarios that cause problems and how they could be reframed.

Change the script

Scene 1

Adult: Your room is a disgrace. Go and tidy it now.

Child: Not now, I'm watching a good programme.

Adult: Did you hear me? I said do it now.

Child: No, I don't want to.

Adult: Do it now or you're grounded for a week.

Child: I don't care.

Adult: Don't you speak to me like that!

Child: Leave me alone. You're always going on at me!

Scene 2

Teacher: I've asked for silence, why are you still talking?

Pupil: It wasn't just me.

Teacher: Be quiet and get on with your work.

Pupil: Stop picking on me. It's not fair.

Teacher: Look, you're disturbing everyone else. Be quiet.

Pupil: Well, don't tell me off and not the others.

Teacher: I don't want to have to speak to you again.

Pupil: Why should I be quiet when you're not being fair!

Teacher: Right, you can stay in at break and talk to me then.

Pupil: No, I won't, because I'm leaving now. *(walks out of the room)*

Scene 3

Child A: Hey, where did you get those shoes? Did you find them in someone's dustbin?

Child B: No, they're new. My mum got them for me.

Child A: I think your mum left her glasses at home when she chose them.

Child C: Yeah, or they were all she could afford.

Child B: They're OK. Just leave me alone.

Child C: Anyway, those shoes match the rest of your useless outfit.

Child B: I said go away!

Child A: Ooh, he said 'Go away'. That's really scary.

Child C: I'm quaking in my cool shoes!

Child A: Go away or else what?

Child C: Yeah, what exactly?

Child B loses their temper and lashes out at child A and child C.

Teacher (to child B): Stop that at once. What do you think you are doing? Go and stand outside the headteacher's room.

© *Helping Children Deal with Anger* LDA Permission to Photocopy

A new classmate

This story is about two animals called Mig and Caz who go to Oak Wood School.

Mig and Caz were best friends. They sat next to each other in class, they played together, ate their lunches together and met up after school.

Caz and Mig liked to do the same things. They shared their toys, played chase and invented all sorts of games. They were such good friends that they hardly ever argued.

One day a new animal called Rik came to their school. Rik joined Mig and Caz's class. Their teacher asked all of them to take care of Rik, who was looking very nervous.

At playtime, Mig noticed that Rik was standing on one side and looking lonely. 'Oh dear,' thought Mig, 'poor Rik looks sad.' Mig went over and began to chat about where Rik had lived before and what Oak Wood was like.

Rik was pleased to have someone to talk to. After a while, Mig said, 'Shall we play a game?'

'Oh yes, please,' said Rik.

Caz found Mig and Rik playing and hurried over. 'I've been looking for you everywhere, Mig. Come and play with my new ball.'

'Not now,' panted Mig. 'I'm playing with Rik. Why don't you join in?'

Caz did not want to join in their game or share Mig with anyone else.

'No, come on, Mig,' Caz said firmly. 'I want you to play with me.'

Mig was surprised at Caz's grumpy tone. 'Let's play together and make friends with Rik. It's nice to have friends to play with and not feel lonely, especially if you're new.'

'Well, I don't care if Rik doesn't have any friends. You're my friend and I want you to come and play with me now!' shouted Caz, red in the face.

Mig was shocked. 'What's got into you? If we play together Rik won't be left out.'

'You don't care about me at all!' Caz shouted and marched off.

After play, Caz ignored Mig. It was the same at lunchtime and after school. Every time Mig tried to make friends, Caz shouted, 'Go and play with your new friend!' Mig was miserable. He still liked Caz and couldn't understand why Caz was so angry. Caz was miserable too. He wanted to be friends with Mig, but couldn't stop feeling angry.

The teacher noticed how miserable Caz and Mig were and asked Mig what was wrong. Mig told her everything. 'Oh dear,' the teacher said. 'Let's see if we can sort this out so that everyone is happy.'

© Helping Children Deal with Anger LDA

Permission to Photocopy

CONCLUSION

Anger can be seen as a natural response to frustration or threat. This discovery will probably have amazed many of your children as this programme may have been the first time that they have thought about this powerful emotion.

By the time you have worked through the sessions in this book, your children will have a better understanding of the causes and effects of anger on both themselves and others. They will also have an insight into what particular incidents arouse anger in themselves and the knowledge that they need not be powerless victims of an overwhelming and potentially destructive force.

This does not, of course, mean that angry responses of a negative manner will be banished from your school for ever. That would be wishful thinking. However, by continuing to remind children of what they have learnt about anger, you can help them to understand how to manage their emotions and develop different responses. As the children see the effectiveness of these responses in achieving a more positive outcome, they will be encouraged to maintain them.

For a few children, learning to control their anger will be a very difficult challenge. They will need a lot of encouragement and frequent praise when they do get it right. You can show them that you understand how hard it is for them to do the right thing and how proud of them you are when they manage to achieve it.

Creating a positive ethos in your school requires an on-going commitment from members of staff to model and encourage appropriate behaviour. If you want to make your school a safer place, you have to maintain this attention throughout successive terms and years. In the busy world of education, it is all too easy to produce short-lived campaigns that are soon replaced by the next focus.

It is, of course, impossible to maintain the same level of interest in any one area indefinitely. However, good practice can become part of your day-to-day experience. If a systematic and consistent approach to anger management is adopted by all the adults in your school, you will have a better chance of influencing and helping your children.

By helping children understand the causes and effects of anger and by teaching them how to manage their emotions more successfully, you will be equipping them with valuable learning for life.

RESOURCES

Mosley, J. (1993) *Turn your School Round*
Mosley, J. (1996) *Quality Circle Time*
Mosley, J. (1998) *More Quality Circle Time*
Mosley, J. (2006) *Using Rewards Wisely*
Mosley, J. and Sonnet, H. (2002) *101 Games for Self-Esteem*
Mosley, J. and Sonnet, H. (2002) *Making Waves*
Mosley, J. and Sonnet, H. (2003) *101 Games for Social Skills*
Mosley, J. and Sonnet, H. (2005) *Better Behaviour through Golden Time*
Mosley, J. and Sonnet, H. (2006) *101 Games for Better Behaviour*
Mosley, J. and Sonnet, H. (2006) *Helping Children Deal with Bullying*
Mosley, J. and Sonnet, H. (2007) *Helping Children Deal with Conflict*
Mosley, J. and Thorp, G. (2005) *Positive Playtimes*

Mosley, J. (2000) *Quality Circle Time in Action*
Mosley, J. (2000) *Quality Circle Time Kit*
Mosley, J. (2004) *Reward Certificates*
Mosley, J. (2005) *Golden Rules Poster*
Mosley, J. (2005) *Lunchtimes Poster Set*
Mosley, J. (2005) *Playground Poster Set*
Mosley, J. (2005) *Playground Stars*
Mosley, J. (2006) *Stickers*

All these resources are published in Cambridge by LDA. For information about the full range of Jenny Mosley's books and resources, please contact LDA Customer Services on 0845 120 4776 or visit our website at www.LDAlearning.com

Training in the Quality Circle Time model

For information about training, contact Jenny Mosley Consultancies:
Telephone: 01225 767157
E-mail: circletime@jennymosley.co.uk
Website: www.circle-time.co.uk
Address: 28a Gloucester Road, Trowbridge, Wiltshire, BA14 0AA